FORM FOLLOWS TECHNIQUE

RICHARD SCHULTZ

SCHIFFER
PUBLISHING

4880 Lower Valley Road · Atglen, PA 19310

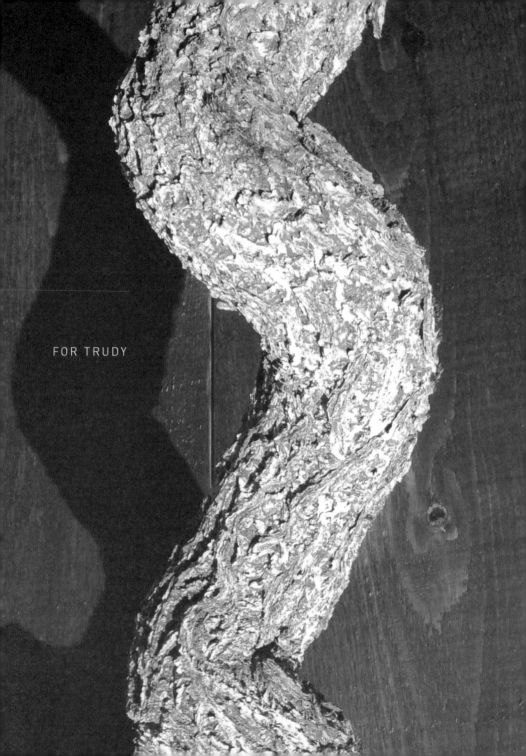

FOR TRUDY

FOREWORD

BY BRIAN LUTZ

The theme of this book took shape as a lecture that Richard Schultz first presented as a way of teaching salespeople how design happens. Schultz, a 1951 graduate of Chicago's Institute of Design, was part of the first wave of practitioners of industrial design, groomed in the tenets of the Modern Era, and committed to stripping away decoration and artifice in search of a rationale, if not a meaning, for form. Inspiration was redefined as a reductive process; less became more, and form, it was said, became a factor of function alone.

But this was hardly a static situation; modernism itself was, in fact, the "vision in motion" that László Moholy-Nagy described in the title of his seminal publication, which became the revered reference text of all Institute of Design students. In the late 1940s the motion at the core of Moholy's premise was a matter of evolving science and technology, and in a welcome turn the expanding world of postwar technology provided designers a new vocabulary, one of humanist possibilities, liberating them from the aesthetic formalism of modernism.

The techniques of postwar production moved quickly in response to innovations in materials evolution and technical understanding of designers. The dogma of the "Form Follows Function" era was more clearly perceived to be a matter of form following the culture of science and social order. Richard Schultz was fortunate enough to be part of this new thinking. As an active participant in the design and development of new products from the late 1940s onward, he observed that form was actually following the technical revolution taking place.

Form Follows Technique is Richard Schultz's personal view of the creative endeavors of humans interacting with the elements of their world—wood, metal, and stone—absent the boundaries of time or culture. Design surrounds us, in form and technique.

INTRODUCTION

A honeysuckle vine wraps itself around a sassafras sapling. The vine dies and the sapling grows but is restrained by the dead vine. We think we see a twisted trunk. What we in fact see is a trunk with a form dictated by a restraint. It is nature's "infallible technique." Nature's method of espalier!

In this book, my purpose is to show how simple techniques, applied consistently, have inspired modern design. We start with chairs. Their function has been the same for centuries. Their form has changed along with the materials and techniques available to their designers. We conclude with several buildings and other structures. All are examples of creativity, utility, and beauty emerging from the application of "infallible" techniques.

DEVELOP AN INFALLIBLE TECHNIQUE

AND THEN PUT YOURSELF AT THE MERCY OF INSPIRATION.

ZEN MAXIM

WOOD

As one of the earliest objects that people have made for themselves, the chair offers an excellent example of how advances in materials and techniques affected the creation of new forms.

Let's start with wood, one of the first materials used to make chairs. It is fairly easy to form using rather simple tools. In fact, a log that is the right height is all one needs for a very minimal chair or stool. The method of working wood that involves the least skill is carving, a process of subtraction. No joinery needed. African craftsmen did some remarkable things with form, which transformed the chair into a sculpture— or did they make sculpture to sit on?

The invention of the saw allowed craftsmen to produce thin pieces or sticks. These sticks could be modified or shaped so that one piece could fit into a hole in another. If the fit was snug, it produced a joint. The hole is named a mortise, and the piece inserted is a tenon.

Using this method, some very elegant chairs have been made, particularly the Windsor chair. The first ones were made in England in the early 1700s. Craftsmen developed a way to use steam to soften and bend wood, which led them to make the Windsor's characteristic curved back. Perhaps it was an effort to copy nature, where curved sticks can be found easily but no two are the same. A good craftsman develops methods that evolve into techniques that can produce nearly identical parts that will fit together to become, in this case, chairs that have the same form.

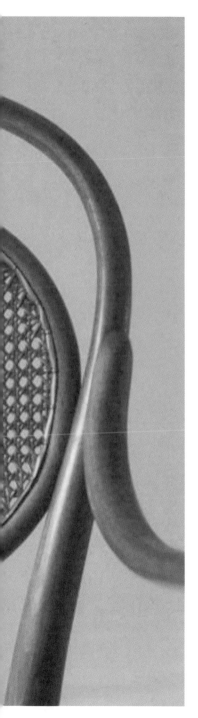

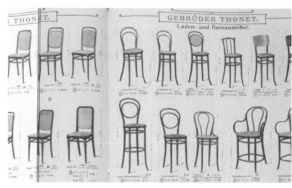

In the 1830s in Germany, Michael Thonet developed the technique of steam-bending wood into an industrial process. By 1841, he had the ability to bend a stick of wood in more than one plane. This gave him a technique that allowed great freedom of form and design. Instead of a mortise-and-tenon joint, he could arrange to have an arm, for example, flow alongside a chair back and be fixed with a screw. In this way, he was able to make designs that seemed to flow together, giving an effect never before seen in a piece of furniture. Form follows technique.

Thonet's catalogue, above, shows the great freedom of design the bentwood technique allowed. It also allowed a freedom to embellish the ends of the bent pieces.

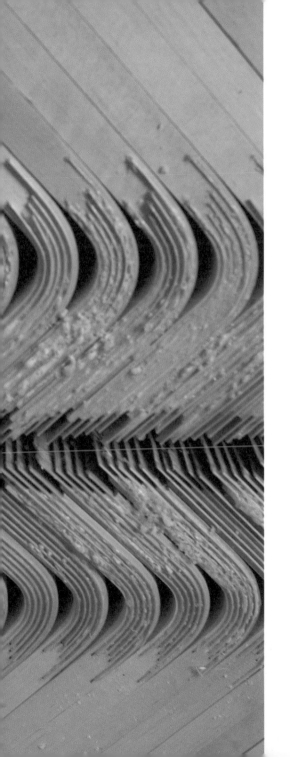

The next innovation was developed in Scandinavia in 1933. Alvar Aalto, an architect in Finland, realized that he could take many thin strips of wood and glue them together on a curved form. This is basically taking a board apart and gluing it back together again to give it a new form. The result is a strong and elastic piece of wood. Aalto laminated the strips, using a form shaped like a chair frame. He conceived various postures for the frame to serve different uses—dining, lounging, and with and without arms.

The frame at right was in the form of what engineers call a cantilever, giving the frame a springy quality that is pleasant to sit on. The surface one sits on is similar to the thin strips that the frame is made from, which gives the chair an integrity that is very pleasing. This kind of consistency of thinking about design took the place of applied form or decoration that characterized design up to the early 1900s. Since the early twentieth century, the emphasis has been on invention, not on copying the past. We will see that this attitude can be described as "form follows technique."

Laminating wood, if the pieces are large enough, could produce a seat, or a back, or a seat and a back together. This was then set into the laminated frames. What could not be done was to make a contoured seat or a contoured back. As a result, these designs were elegant looking but not comfortable. They were not mass produced as were the webbed chairs.

What finally happened with laminated wood was due to a new technique developed by Charles Eames in California in 1946. During World War II, the Eames office worked to develop splints for arm and leg injuries using laminated wood. Because the splint needed to fit the human body, it had to be curved, and in solving this problem Eames developed a technique for laminating wood that was more sophisticated than Aalto needed.

At about this time the Museum of Modern Art in New York conducted a low-cost furniture competition. Eames developed a chair (following page) by using the methods he had employed for the splints. It was very comfortable.

The shape of the seat and back was carefully designed to avoid compound bends, which laminated wood cannot be made to do. I remember sitting in one of these chairs in 1946 and being very impressed with the comfort. The back was fixed to the frame with a flexible rubber mounting, which was brilliant. Wooden chairs had come a long way through innovations in technique.

IN ART, PROGRESS LIES NOT IN AN
EXTENSION BUT IN A KNOWLEDGE OF
LIMITATIONS. THE LIMITATIONS OF A
METHOD SECURE ITS STYLE, ENGENDER
NEW FORM, AND LEAD TO CREATION.

GEORGES BRAQUE

METAL

The use of metal in chair construction was almost unheard of until steel tubing was recognized as having aesthetic possibilities.

Marcel Breuer, who was at the German design school called the Bauhaus, is said to have been inspired by the handlebars on his bicycle. In 1928 he made the Cesca chair (*right*) using tubing to produce a springy frame to which he attached a wooden cane seat and back. The first chairs were made by the Thonet company of bentwood fame. The technique of bending steel tubing is very different from steam-bending or laminating wood, however.

The design of the chair shows this. A tube bender wraps a piece of tubing around a mandrel and makes a bend that has the same radius as the mandrel. Because of the limits of the machine, another bend cannot be made directly next to the first bend. Accordingly, bent-tube designs consist of bends connected by straight sections— quite different from steam-bent wood pieces. Form follows technique.

The form of tubular designs, of course, can vary depending on the tooling used. Mies van der Rohe designed this chair in 1927. It has quite a different feeling than the Breuer chair and uses a simple piece of leather for the seating surface, which is in nice contrast to the machine-like quality of the tubing. Both chairs have the springy comfort that the cantilevered tubing makes possible. The appeal of these designs is the elementary simplicity: a design from which nothing can be taken away and to which nothing needs to be added.

The basic understanding about wire is that it is a tension material. To try to use it in compression is foolish. This was my first thought when seeing this old design based on wire in compression. It works, however!

The twisting produces a strong leg, and at the top of the legs the wires spread out to form a strong triangle where they are bolted to the seat frame. The stretcher threads through the twisted leg very cleverly and ties the legs together. There is no welding at this point. The edge of the seat is made of a steel angle formed into a circle. The seat fits into it. The back is minimal and springy. The wire is just the correct hardness to be both stiff and springy where needed. The assembly of these chairs is easy because the wire is flexible enough to allow assembly of parts that may not be made to exact specifications. The feet are to be admired, since they do not require the addition of any other metal part. The top of the back is a loop, as is the foot!

The Eames office developed a wire chair that was based on the technique of welding wire used in the construction of wire baskets. This involves welding a wire grid by using a method that makes all the welds at once. It results in a flat wire grid that can then be folded to produce a basket, as we are familiar with at the supermarket.

When this wire grid has a rim around its edge, it cannot be formed into a contoured shape. Eames produced a grid with many unwelded wires extending from all four sides. When this grid was bent to produce a chair-like shape, the areas that would be most contoured at the sides were free to bend without distortion.

This welded assembly was then put into a jig, and two preformed wire rims were welded onto the loose ends of the seat's wires. The projecting wire ends were then sheared off. This is a good example of Braque's talk about the limitations of a method securing its style.

The Knoll furniture company assigned me to work with Harry Bertoia from 1952 to 1953 to help him design and develop his chairs made from welded wire. He was a sculptor who worked directly in the material: wire. Harry made no drawings or models. He made a seat from plywood panels that could be adjusted to give the best comfort. Sitting on this, he began to sketch in space with lengths of wire to establish the outer portions of a seat. He then added more wire to establish a continuous surface for the seat and back.

He attached the wires using a torch and brazing wire. As this curved surface grew, he would sometimes use a mallet to change the contour. As Harry added more wires, we saw that the configuration began forming a grid, a sort of diamond shape.

Harry was not a man of many words, and I do not remember discussing the work at length. He was a very hard worker; sometimes when I came into the shop the next morning there would be more chair there than the day before. As he worked, I would prebend a wire for him based on what the next step seemed to be. So far, what we had was a sketch in wire that sat on the plywood armature. No base yet. Since the wires were running diagonally, that started to determine the shape of the chair, or basket, as we called it. The shape emerged organically from the process—or technique—of making a surface by welding wires in a diagonal pattern. It was a diamond.

What was not there were any kind of arms—only a seat and back surface. The portion that became the arms was formed by shaping the basket with the mallet. At this point we needed to make another basket that would be much less crude and more symmetrical. We wanted to arrange the wires in an orderly manner.

We did this by turning the basket upside down and building another one over the first. This was done by forming wires to fit over the outside. Unlike the first version, where the surface grew organically as we added wire, this time we started by bending a wire to establish a border first, copying the original but making it symmetrical. Working this way, we produced another basket that was starting to look much more like a finished product.

When we sat in it, we found where it had to be enlarged or changed to achieve a comfortable shape. At one point, we decided we needed to make the whole chair a little bigger. To do so, we built another basket on the outer surface of the first one.

Eventually we had what looked and felt like a basket one could sit in. But was it a chair? There was no base.

Harry then designed a base that fitted onto the sides of the basket so that it was suspended, putting the wire in tension rather than compression. The joints of the base were the same crosswire welds, made with the same machine, as the welds in the basket.

Finally, we had made a chair that had a comfortable shape and showed promise. Sitting on the textured grid for a long time, though, diminished the comfort; we felt the need for a cushion or pad. We developed both a seat pad and a pad that covered the entire basket. This required the development of a laminated cover of fabric and foam that had the form and contour of the basket and could be held in place without snaps or buttons, unlike standard slipcovers.

While I was working on that project, Harry started on variations of the diamond shape. A larger diamond version was next. It was mounted on the base using a flexible rubber connector that allowed the basket to move or rock as the sitter moved. He also made a chair that had a headrest. This too was attached to the base with rubber mounts. Now that he had the first chair developed, it was easy to do these variations because he had invented a technique that worked well.

Next, Harry designed an armless dining chair, which gave him the most trouble because it was not based on the diamond shape. A new form had to be developed. During the weeks, months, and years that all this design work was going on, Harry would come into the shop in the evening and work on sculpture. In the end the whole Knoll showroom was filled with Harry's work—furniture and sculpture—a sensational show!

Sheet metal can be bent into complex
shapes by using expensive tooling, but
starting with the basic folds or bends
that can be made in paper or cardboard
limits the design to simpler forms. As
I built shapes out of cardboard for the
designs on these pages, the simplest
way to support the chair was to let the
arm and leg be one piece of material, so
the arm extends naturally to the ground.
The resulting designs can be made
using the tools in any sheet metal shop.

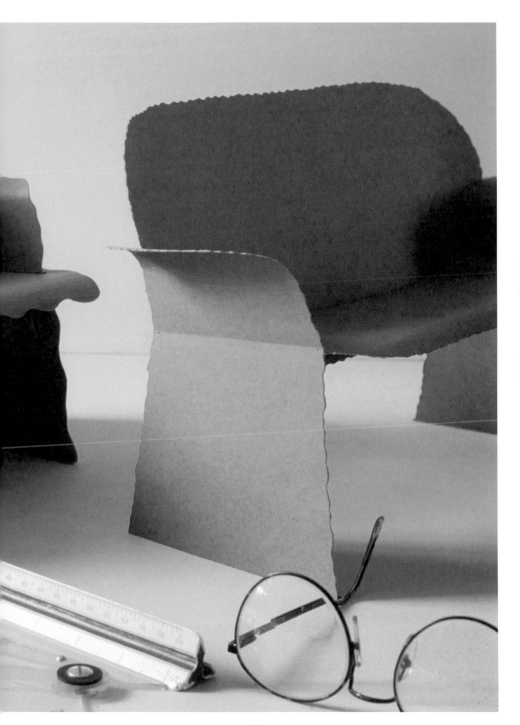

These designs also emerge from the standard techniques of making holes in paper with a metal punch and mallet, and shaping the edges of a sheet with scissors. Using a simple round punch but overlapping the holes allowed more complex holes to emerge. As I thought about a design for outdoor use, I found these holes might imitate shadows cast by foliage.

This furniture was designed for the garden. It is made of aluminum to resist rusting and, if painted green, seems to imitate shrubbery. It is called Topiary—a shrub trimmed to resemble a seat.

These chairs, *at left*, stack. The panel leg does not allow that to happen, but the tubular leg does. As can be seen, the holes can be any shape. In this case it is a decorative decision, as is the outer shape of the panels, which have little to do with comfort.

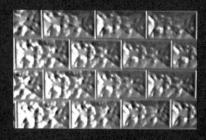

I found sheet metal embossed with
a pattern of hewn stone laid up in
courses. This material looks like
solid stone, but isn't. I find it amusing
because it contradicts so vividly the
phrase "truth to materials" which
modern designers hold dear. I
designed a pyramid with an exposed
corner detail which reveals the true
nature of the sheet metal.

PLASTIC

All we have said about form following technique leaves out an important point. The techniques and their limitations that we have been discussing provide a pathway to something pleasing. If you have a feeling for wood, as did Aalto, you will find inspiration in the laminating process. If you immerse yourself in welding, you will be inspired, as was Bertoia, to construct a seat using that method. The Zen maxim says it all: "Develop an infallible technique and then put yourself at the mercy of inspiration."

However, these techniques do not guarantee good design. The forms that result from these techniques also depend on the judgment of the maker. The Saarinen chair demonstrates this point. Probably the most talented architect of midcentury America, Eero Saarinen was trained as an architect in America and as a sculptor in France. He spoke of himself as a form-giver.

A friend of mine who worked with Saarinen was shown how to make a form by building up clay on an armature, as did sculptors such as Rodin. This was how the shape of these chairs was developed.

Saarinen knew that the chairs would be made of fiberglass and polyester plastic in a mold. But the mold could be almost any shape and was not a factor in constraining the form except that the finished shape must be easily removable . . . no undercuts. To go back to Braque, this is a method for which

there are less obvious limitations. What makes these chairs successful is the skill and talent of a master form-giver.

However, Saarinen was a rarity. And plastics and resins are unusually versatile. While all designers must ultimately take up the role of form-givers, many will find inspiration from working with materials that present more-natural constraints and developing techniques specific to those limits.

Now let's look beyond chairs to larger structures. The form-giver could be a stone mason or a Japanese builder—we will see beautiful forms emerge from consistently applied techniques.

STONE

The well-known fieldstone wall in America can be visually very pleasing but does not emerge from a consistent technique. Each stone is hand selected and fitted into place. The result is that such a wall cannot usually be made very high.

ARCHITECTURE BEGINS
WHEN ONE BRICK IS PLACED
CAREFULLY ON ANOTHER.

MIES VAN DER ROHE

On my first trip to Japan, I was delighted to see a simple solution: a method so obviously the answer to the problem. After arranging the very first row in a sort of sawtooth pattern, the succeeding rows have a place to fit in this nesting arrangement. The Japanese even take the next step and make cast cement blocks to be laid up in a similar pattern, which has the stability of the diagonal orientation. Form follows technique!

SHELTER

One of the most elementary ways to construct a shelter is to use posts with beams spanning from post to post. What then can be done is to somehow fill in the space created to produce a wall. This was done in Denmark centuries ago with a technique in which small stones are piled up in a wood frame and then coated with a kind of wash of limestone or plaster. This nineteenth-century barn, made in this method, has been moved from an island east of Copenhagen to the Open Air Museum near Copenhagen. There are many other vernacular buildings there, so one can see how early structures were made.

What is interesting for the purpose of our argument is that a very similar technique has been used in Japan for centuries and has resulted in structures that are remarkably similar to those from Denmark in their shape and aesthetic appeal. While there could have been no communication between the builders, the method prevailed. This is a remarkable example of form following technique.

The Katsura Imperial Villa, built in 1615, is one of the most beautiful buildings in the world. Its appeal derives from the extremely minimal means used to make it—the post-and-beam system—because it is made using a modular system based on the dimensions of the tatami mat (approximately 3 × 6 feet). It is also very minimally decorated or embellished. This allows the proportions to, in a sense, dominate the design.

Nothing so elegantly minimal as this
was done in the West until Mondrian.
The aesthetics of Japan remained
unappreciated by European art
historians for a very long time. When
Walter Gropius, the founder of the
Bauhaus, visited Katsura he said that
the aesthetic that it represented is what
he had been striving for all his life.

Think about what Pablo Casals said
about performing music: freedom
within great order.

AFTERWORD

An alternative title for this work could have been How to Understand Design. I wanted to avoid making a statement about aesthetics. I have not always been successful. I did use words like "pleasing" or "elegant" or "feeling." These are words that help describe what results from pursuing a consistent technique. But as we said when talking about Saarinen, following a technique does not guarantee arriving at a good design. The technique is the starting point. You develop a feeling for what can be done and what should be done when you are working with a material. This is what Aalto did working with laminates and what Bertoia did working with wire. The limitations of a method are oftentimes the source of creativity. As Georges Braque says, "Build on a knowledge of the limitations of a method."

What is also important to know is that none of the seating discussed here, from the African stools to my own chairs, was done to satisfy the demands of a market. There was no market for such designs. There was no style that existed that architects and designers were trying to fit into. But, in the modern era at least, there was something in the air: a zeitgeist that existed and could be felt by those working at the time. There was a great sense of optimism. We lived in the present and we were inventing it as we went along. What I have tried to do in this book is write down some of what we all understood as to how to work as designers. I hope you will find the same inspiration as you find a technique that you can make your own.

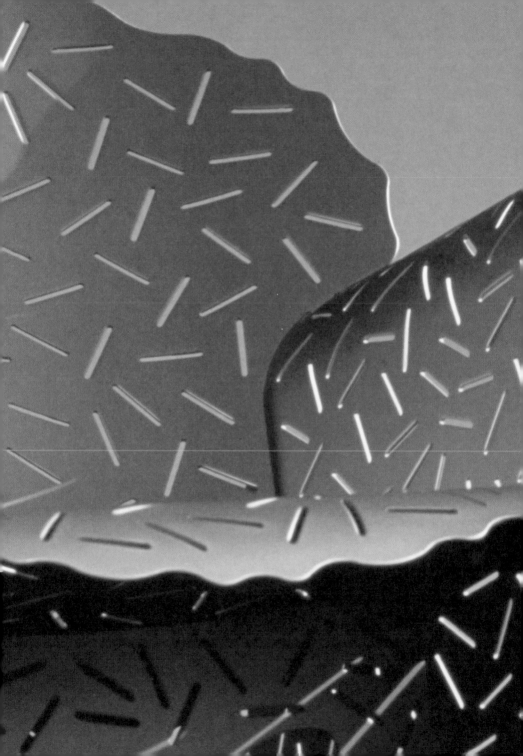

Other Schiffer Books on Related Subjects:
David N. Ebner: Studio Furniture, Nancy Schiffer,
ISBN 978-0-7643-4414-5
Knoll Home & Office Furniture, Nancy Schiffer,
ISBN 978-0-7643-2395-9
The Life and Work of Harry Bertoia: The Man, the Artist, the Visionary, Celia Bertoia, ISBN 978-0-7643-4693-4

Library of Congress Control Number: 2019936843

Designed by Laura Eitzen

Type set in SapientSans

ISBN: 978-0-7643-5819-7
Printed in China

Published by Schiffer Publishing, Ltd.
4880 Lower Valley Road
Atglen, PA 19310
Phone: (610) 593-1777; Fax: (610) 593-2002
E-mail: Info@schifferbooks.com
Web: www.schifferbooks.com

For our complete selection of fine books on this and related subjects, please visit our website at www.schifferbooks.com. You may also write for a free catalog.

Schiffer Publishing's titles are available at special discounts for bulk purchases for sales promotions or premiums. Special editions, including personalized covers, corporate imprints, and excerpts, can be created in large quantities for special needs. For more information, contact the publisher.

We are always looking for people to write books on new and related subjects. If you have an idea for a book, please contact us at proposals@schifferbooks.com.

PHOTO CREDITS:

Ilan Rubin	Front Cover
David Kelly Crow	Rear Cover
Shutterstock	Pages 6–7
Collection RMCA Tervuren; photo H. Schneebeli, MRAC Tervuren ©	Pages 8–9
Courtesy of Artek, photo André Demony	Pages 18–19
Courtesy of Artek	Pages 20–21
Courtesy of Artek	Page 22
Courtesy of Herman Miller	Pages 24–25
Courtesy of Knoll, Inc.	Page 28
Courtesy of Knoll, Inc.	Page 29
Ilan Rubin	Pages 30–31
Courtesy of Herman Miller	Page 34
Hub Wilson	Page 48
Ilan Rubin	Pages 52–53
Courtesy of Knoll, Inc.	Page 54
Courtesy of Knoll, Inc.	Page 55
Shutterstock	Pages 56–57

GRAMMARIAN:
Steven Schultz

INSPIRATION:
Trudy Schultz

A very special thanks to Laura Eitzen, whom I have known all her life, who made this book as elegant as it is.